Asshats to Assets:
How to Turn Crappy Jobs into Career Gold

by Wendy Dwyer

Contents

*With much love and gratitude, this book is dedicated
to my students and colleagues at Indian River State College
and all the bosses and co-workers – good and bad,
asshats and assets – who have helped me learn.*

*It is also dedicated with much love and respect
to my beloved husband, Daniel Hafner,
all the critters at Jakewood
who kept me company while I wrote,
my parents, Richard and Coraljean,
and my fourteen angels
who always believe in me when I doubt myself.*

Asshat

One who has his head up his ass,

thus wearing his ass as a hat...

Instead of sticking their heads in the sand,

they have instead opted to stick them up their asses.

Urban Dictionary

Prologue

Why should you listen to me?

I've been a puppet, a pauper, a pirate,

a poet, a pawn, and a king.

I've been up and down and over and out,

and I know one thing.

Each time I find myself flat on my face,

I pick myself up and get back in the race.

Dean Kay and Kelly Gordon via Frank Sinatra

It would be so much simpler if I could just tell you I was "born this way" and usher you into my palatial mansion, so we could sit by the infinity pool and drink mimosas while I share the wisdom I want you to think I was born possessing like an aura of brilliance and success hovering around me. Unfortunately, I would be lying to you, and though I am good at a whole bunch of useless things, I am a terrible liar. I can't drink more than one mimosa either, so let's just cut to the chase and be real with one another.

You're here because you want to learn if that crappy job you're in is ever going to benefit you. I'm here because I can help you. Aside from the meager paycheck and a rock solid excuse to keep you from being the go-to guy or gal to drive all of your more successful friends and family members to the airport for their next vacations, that job you're in may be feeling more like a noose slowly tightening around your neck.

I get it. I've been there, too, and my list of crappy jobs and asshat bosses reads like a *Top Ten List of Employment Disasters.*

I've been a chambermaid (the one who changes the sheets in the hotel room you and your buddies rented on that wild spring break that year), an answering service operator, a radio 'personality,' a donut shop clerk, a police dispatcher, a secretary, an administrative assistant, choir director (barely read music), and a marketing manager.

But wait, there's more. I've also been a survey representative (the one who asks you if you put meat in your spaghetti sauce and what brand of laundry soap you prefer).

In another life, I worked as an advocate for the developmentally disabled, a waitress, ski condition reporter (I don't ski and am a klutz of epic proportions), a convenience store clerk, tutor, lead singer, party motivator (one who is invited to the parties because of their ability to improve every party), photographer, house sitter, foreign language software tester (I speak exceedingly limited French, but tested Thai software), volunteer coordinator, special events manager, writer, and college professor. There are others, too, but I think you're getting the idea.

And if the idea you're getting is that I'm a job-hopper, you're getting the wrong idea. Yes, I have a storied career path, but with a couple of exceptions, I left each job on my own with a gift or asset I took to the subsequent positions.

And that's exactly what I hope to share with you. For every crummy work experience, bosshole, or asshat I've endured, I've also learned valuable tools, made phenomenal connections, and gained wisdom, skills, and experience in ways I never imagined possible.

What's in it for You?

In addition to enjoying a rollicking journey of adventure and screw-ups in someone else's career history (mine), you'll have a chance to learn from my mistakes (and successes) to help you save time, frustration, and possible therapy bills. I want you to succeed, of course, but I also want you to find a career that you love and work that makes you feel good about yourself and the world. We all know far too many people who are miserable, who wish away their weekdays, or who anesthetize themselves because they hate their jobs and subsequently their lives.

I don't want that to be you, so I'm here to show you that you can accomplish great things in your career and life, be happy, and maintain your sense of humor without selling your soul. Best of all, to do all that, you don't have to be:

- Incredibly talented

- Breathtakingly beautiful

- Exceptionally educated

- Supremely connected

- Extremely wealthy

All you have to be is yourself and have some ambition. It also helps if you are a good listener, are not a narcissist, are willing to learn, and have a sense of humor. If you think you can handle that order (which I hope is not asking too much), then shall we begin to help you turn asshats into assets and crappy jobs into career gold?

Chapter 1

Why Do I Have to Start at the Bottom?

Every spring, in my capacity as a college professor, I invite a group of thirty local leaders of business and industry to participate in a speed dating event. Okay, it is not really speed dating in the traditional sense because nobody 'hooks up' or ends up married because of it, but if you know the premise of speed dating, it will make explaining what I do a lot easier. Studies have shown that the average attention span of a goldfish is approximately nine seconds, and the attention span of the average human being is currently only seven seconds. Aside from being horrifying information to learn at any age, finding this out inspired me to create a one-day event I called "Speed Communicating."

You see, if it only takes seven seconds for us to lose our attention span, that means we only have seven seconds to make a first impression – good or bad. So every spring, I invite business and industry leaders to come and facilitate very brief, 12-minute mini-workshops on a variety of different topics designed to give college students and members of the community who are looking to improve their job skills and life hacks to help them make a great and lasting first impression.

Topics at the annual event include what to wear to make a good first impression, how to tackle difficult questions, how to impress on a Skype interview, how to find a volunteer gig that will help build skills and credibility, how to shake hands and maintain eye contact that isn't creepy, the importance of punctuality, how to make social media work to your advantage, and several other offerings.

After this year's event, participants and facilitators alike were super-excited and feeling very inspired by the cogent questions posed and the amount of helpful, real-life information they were able to give and receive in twelve tiny minutes per topic.

As always, I asked if there were any topics the facilitators would like to see offered the next time the event occurs. And for the first time ever, business owners, hiring managers, and even non-profit professionals asked for the same thing. All of them wanted a workshop to deal with the importance of starting at the bottom in the process of becoming a highly-regarded, super sought-after professional.

"I hire someone right out of college," said one human resource manager, "and within a month, he's in my office asking me when he can expect to be promoted to the head of a department or division. It's crazy, but it happens all the time now," she lamented. "The employee has barely figured out the nuances of the office copy machine, and he thinks he's ready to take on the entire boardroom!"

Another nodded his head furiously in agreement. "Right!" he exclaimed. "Last week I had a new staff member tell me he didn't really need to take on a project that involved collecting data because, and I'm not making this up, he said he'd already done a spreadsheet already and wanted a new challenge."

While it's true that your education is tremendously valuable and the semesters you spent slogging through classes that you never imagined would have any bearing whatsoever on 'real life' actually did help prepare you for the 'real world,' it's also true that the best way to learn how to scale a mountain is to start at the bottom. Not only will you get the satisfaction of knowing that you did it from start to finish, you'll be amazed at the experience and skills you pick up along the way.

Starting at the bottom of your field or on the lowest rung of the corporate ladder is nothing to be ashamed of. After all, didn't you learn how to crawl before you took off running? And I would bet my first paycheck that you probably used training wheels before you figured out a way to ride a two-wheeler and then tackle riding no-handed, right?

Starting at the bottom isn't the worst thing; it's the first thing in business success. And it has some pretty awesome benefits too, though truth be told, it sometimes can feel like your amazing skills and talents aren't being properly recognized. The most useful thing about starting at the bottom is the view – yes, the view.

When you accept a position at the bottom of the corporate ladder, you have the best vantage point to see asshats in action. Why is seeing asshats in action such a valuable asset to your career, you ask? It's simple – when you watch someone doing something offensive, rude, inconsiderate, unprofessional, or simply stupid, you tend to learn just as much as you would if you were the one making those dumb mistakes and attempting to sabotage your own credibility and career.

From your lowly and humble spot at the bottom of the corporate later, it may look and smell a bit like asshats for a good reason – where else will you ever have such a clear view and perspective of what's happening 'up top' than from underneath it?

Though the only skill I possess on a pair of downhill skis is to stand helplessly by the lodge, praying for the day to be over so I can get to the hot cocoa part of the day, it is true that once upon a time, I was the voice of downhill skiing for an entire state – and a big state, too. The job involved working overnight, recording snowfall and condition data from over 50 ski resorts and areas from around the country, then creating approximately 25 unique radio-ready ski reports for different geographic areas and media outlets around the state.

Despite being a monumental task at any time of day, doing this job in the dead of night with a morning radio drive time deadline looming large was a challenge, and it was always a treat to collect the paycheck - until the week when there wasn't a paycheck, that is. The newly-hired director of the operation was a dashing, young man, fresh out of the frat house and in the Executive Director position of an association created and funded by all the ski areas throughout the state to promote their business and tourism opportunities involving skiing. It was a heady job for a guy who was still learning that it's not really okay to grab your crumpled clothes from last night off the floor and don them quickly before dashing out the door of your apartment in order to make it to work on time and play 'executive.'

Making the transition from frat boy to junior executive was particularly difficult for this youngster, who had a very healthy ego but who'd had to shoulder very little responsibility in life, fiscal or otherwise. When he found that he wasn't able to live the lifestyle to which he'd become accustomed in college on the meager paycheck as a newbie CEO, this charming asshat decided to borrow from the company fund discreetly by withholding the paychecks of the rest of the staff. He knew that the paychecks would bounce because he'd dipped the organization's bank balance so low with his own withdrawals, so he simply didn't distribute them to the employees.

Needless to say, this technique did not work for a long period of time, but it was a teachable moment for me – bleary-eyed and holding my nose at the muddy base of a particularly smelly corporate ladder.

In most other businesses, such foolishness would get caught and dealt with before employees had a chance to see it happening, but in a small, non-profit association with one central office in a big state and very little oversight, it was a supremely effective way to learn how easily someone can make a foolish novice mistake and ruin his credit and credibility – possibly for life. Within weeks, our cocky young executive was out on the street, our paychecks had resumed their consistent arrival, and people were happily being reminded every morning on their way to work that, "Trail conditions change constantly, so please try to always remember to be aware and ski with care."

Chapter 1 – Nuggets

- Don't be disappointed or discouraged if you have to start from the bottom. Be glad because that's where you learn the most. Whether it's figuring out how to make the photocopier do magical things that amaze your supervisors or learning how not to embezzle from the company, there's plenty to learn from the vantage point at the bottom. Think of it as the base camp for your climb to greatness, and rock the bottom rung.

- As nice as it would be, there's a good chance no one is going to ask you to be the CEO at your first job. If they do, you should run for your life because you're not ready, and they are clinically insane. That ringing in your ears is the sound of warning bells. Listen up. Usually, you start at the bottom because that's the only option available, and besides, it's the best place to watch and learn how to climb and where the best places to lodge your grappling hook will be found.

- Enjoy it at the bottom. It might seem lowly and humbling, and that's not a bad thing to learn from the start of your journey.

- It would probably be a good idea for all of us to strive to at least have the attention span of a goldfish.

- In skiing, downhill and cross-country trail conditions actually do change constantly, so please do remember to "be aware and ski with care."

Chapter 2

What Skills Can I Really Learn from the Asshats?

Every morning for a period of three years, the office asshat, a junior executive, would call out from his wood-paneled office, "Boy! I sure could go for some hot cocoa." That was my cue to leap from my desk in the reception area and whip up some steaming hot cocoa (two packages of the powdered stuff, mixed expertly with some half-and-half to ensure there were no clumps of powder floating at the top), hand-delivered with a flourish that felt like the corporate version of a curtsey. Every morning, I hated the asshat a little more.

You may argue that if it bothered me so much, I should have confronted the asshat or at the very least spit in his hot cocoa (Eww! never even considered it), and perhaps you've got a point. But the company's owners were great guys – a trio of ex-hippies who'd turned entrepreneurs, and I was a glorified receptionist who'd spent some time living in a Pontiac Phoenix just before the start of winter, so I bit my tongue, made delicious hot cocoa, and dreamed of the day when I would be brave enough to get a tattoo on the inside of my palm with the simple letters J.P.M.

J.P.M. is short for "Just Pay Me," which is the mantra I dreamed up to help me weather the storms of a series of pretty crummy jobs with more than their fair share of asshats.

Whether it was the junior executive who wanted to achieve hot cocoa perfection, the housekeeping supervisor who would rail if the "Sanitized for your protection" strip wasn't facing the right direction on the just-cleaned toilets at the hotel where I was a chambermaid, or the radio station manager having an affair with one of the sales staff who drunkenly called me at 3 a.m. to tell me I was fired before a 5:30 air shift, there never seems to be a shortage of asshats in the workplace.

And while it may be dramatic and very theatrical to imagine delivering a biting speech to the aforementioned asshat ala Jerry Maguire before his bosses got the memo, it's probably not the best career move for you, no matter how great it would feel – for about thirty seconds.

What you can do is take a moment to remind yourself of your own mantra (feel free to borrow JPM), and remember that despite the asshats and humiliating shit you're asked to endure on a daily basis, at least you get a paycheck at the end of the week. There are lots of things you're willing to do for a paycheck, and they aren't all glamorous and filtered with the nicest Instagram glow.

And just as important to remember is that you are getting a hands-on lesson in how not to treat others when you're in charge.

Remember how you felt when you were riding the school bus and the cool kids were mean to some poor schmuck whose parents bought him or her bargain sneakers or a knockoff lunchbox (does anyone even use lunchboxes in the 21st Century)?

When you saw someone being bullied, unless your life was an after school special – and I know it wasn't, it probably took you a time or two before you gathered up the cojones to come to the victim's defense.

And whether you came to the aid of victim or not, I'll bet you still remember the circumstance and how it made you feel. Maybe you still carry around a little shard of guilt or remorse for not having done something, and that's good. It's not good because I want you to feel guilty; it's good because it was a clear, life lesson for you in how not to treat others.

When I was in sixth grade, my teacher decided to recreate Jane Elliott's famous "Blue Eyes/Brown Eyes" experiment in racism and human nature. In our class, it was called "Top Dogs and Underdogs," and those of us who started out as underdogs were not allowed to speak without being invited to do so.

We were also made to wear a badge identifying us as underdogs, and we were at the mercy of the top dogs all through the day. If they told us we weren't allowed to sit down during the lesson, we couldn't argue. We just stood up and felt inferior because that's what we were informed that we were. That day was the last day I felt close to many of the classmates I'd grown up with and shared graham crackers and grape juice with for years.

Throughout the day, I remember thinking that one day, the tables would be turned, and wouldn't it be great to be a top dog – one of the lucky few calling the shots and ordering the others around?

All that afternoon, I wondered if I would act as horridly as so many of my classmates had when given the taste of blood – or preteen power.

What a surprise for two dozen sixth graders when we walked into class the next morning and were instructed that our roles would be reversed, and the underdogs would now be the top dogs with the same rights and privileges as the others had relished the day before.

Immediately, some of my classmates began to order around the kids who'd bullied us on the previous day. As satisfying as exacting severe revenge on the young asshats-in-training may have felt, I just couldn't bring myself to make a demand or put my classmates in an awkward or uncomfortable position. Those who could took on a new look in my eyes, and I never quite saw them through the same lens again. It was the most powerful moment of my education that far and possibly to date.

Little did I know that part of what I was learning was how not to treat others when given the opportunity to be on top. I learned that respect is earned, not doled out randomly or according to eye color. And I learned that while there is some benefit, even in the short term, to being an asshat because it feels so good to be able to call all the shots, in the long run, you're lonely and isolated.

I'm not sure how the legendary evil Prince Machiavelli did it with the whole "better to be feared than loved," schtick, but that management style isn't for me, and I don't think it's effective for too many others, either. That doesn't mean people don't try to follow the Machiavellian lead every day in business and life, but if you look closely, I think you'll find that most of those folks are the asshats who don't get invited to the after-work happy hours and weekend gatherings between friendly co-workers.

And though they may get the few extra bucks in their paycheck, they're often unhappy people who make life difficult for others because they know how much misery loves company.

Opinions are like anuses and asshats – everybody has one or can be one if we choose to do so. It's up to you to decide which path you want to take. How far will you go for a paycheck, and what exactly are the limits of your own JPM mantra? The best thing you can learn from the asshats in your workplace is how not to be and act and how to keep from falling victim to the seductive and intoxicating charms of power – even a little bit of it.

Chapter 2 Nuggets

- The most delicious hot cocoa is made with two packets of the powdered stuff and a shot of half-and-half. Mix them together until absolutely smooth, and add hot, but not boiling water. Deliver with something just short of a curtsey for optimal workplace effect.

- JPM – Just Pay Me is more than a painful hand tattoo. It's a mantra to help you remind yourself that you do need to collect a paycheck, and sometimes that means having to endure the asshats in the workplace.

- JPM is also a good reminder to check your ego and your constitution to figure out what you will and will not endure for a paycheck. How much is too much to take, and what is your deal breaker in what you will do for a paycheck?

- Youv'e heard it before: What goes around comes around...karma is a bitch, and the Golden Rule (Do unto others as you would have them do unto you) are important to remember when someone hands you the keys, and you're in the driver's seat. As great as it would feel to back up the bus and roll over all the asshats who have done you wrong or bruised your ego, remember that one day, the tables will be turned, and you could be back on the bottom again, looking up and knowing a whole lot more than you do now. Use that power wisely, and try to remember to exercise humility.

When JPM doesn't work for me as a mantra, I pull out an old copy of Rudyard Kipling's message to his son, the poem *If* and read it to myself to remind myself the importance of seeing both sides of the coin and keeping myself humble. After all, though we don't like to admit it, everyone has an anus and can act like an asshole – even yours truly. And whether we like to believe it or not about ourselves and our own, all assholes stink.

Bonus gift, courtesy of Rudyard Kipling

If

If you can keep your head when all about you;
Are losing theirs and blaming it on you,
If you can trust yourself when all men doubt you,
But make allowance for their doubting too.
If you can wait and not be tired by waiting,
Or being lied about, don't deal in lies,
Or being hated, don't give way to hating,
And yet don't look too good, nor talk too wise:

If you can dream—
and not make dreams your master;
If you can think—and not make thoughts your aim;
If you can meet with Triumph and Disaster,
And treat those two impostors just the same;
If you can bear to hear the truth you've spoken
Twisted by knaves to make a trap for fools,
Or watch the things you gave your life to, broken,
And stoop and build 'em up with worn-out tools

:

If you can make a heap of all your winnings
And risk it on one turn of pitch-and-toss,
And lose, and start again at your beginnings
And never breathe a word about your loss;
If you can force your heart and nerve and sinew
To serve your turn long after they are gone,
And so hold on when there is nothing in you
Except the Will which says to them: "Hold on!"

If you can talk with crowds and keep your virtue,
Or walk with Kings—nor lose the common touch,
If neither foes nor loving friends can hurt you,
If all men count with you, but none too much;
If you can fill the unforgiving minute
With sixty seconds' worth of distance run,
Yours is the Earth and everything that's in it,
And—which is more—you'll be a Man, my son!

Chapter 3

How do I Deal with a Toxic Work Environment?

Once upon a time, a young, bright, talented, and exceedingly lovely princess – me, (okay, literary license is the bombdiggity!) worked for a local branch of a national nonprofit organization whose mission was, roughly, to pool the donation efforts of community members and businesses to ensure their donation dollars would make a greater community impact. I think my job title was Communications Director, though if you've ever worked for a nonprofit organization, you'll already know that often, fabulous job titles are bestowed upon employees in lieu of fabulous wages. Such was the case here, and it became clear early on that I was not only the Communications Director with no staff to direct but wore many other uncomfortable hats, too.

I spent my days drafting press releases, creating and formatting newsletters, pitching stories and photo opportunities, and shooting more 'grip and grin' photos than any one human should have to see in a single lifetime. Grip and grin photos are the ones where a bunch of people in business attire hold onto a giant cardboard check or shake hands and smile broadly, pretending that they just pulled that giant check out of their back pocket.

Unfortunately, working in an office filled with bosses with inflated titles and self-esteem who mostly lived on SlimFast®, cigarettes, and gossip, I also spent far too much time hoisting the five-gallon water jug onto the water cooler, schlepping the garbage, rearranging tables in the conference room for a variety of meetings, cleaning storerooms, and even repainting the office because...well, because the director didn't want to raise the organization's legendary low overhead percentage by paying a professional painter.

From my office, I could hear the CEO and her BFF, whom she'd gotten a job as the VP of Donor Relations, snickering and sharing 'mean-girl' talk about everyone from donors and community dignitaries to staff members and colleagues. I knew before my performance review that I was going to be written up for wearing jeans and a shirt with holes into work (when painting the office), and I knew that no matter how hard I tried to please these women who were my bosses, it was never going to happen.

As you can imagine, it was a toxic work environment – at least for me. So why am I dredging up an awful work memory and sharing it despite how effectively it paints me as an office doormat? I'm doing it because maybe I can help keep you from making the same mistakes I did and give you a chance to deal more effectively and positively than I did with the toxic workplace. Here's what does *not* work in dealing with a toxic workplace.

Self-medication is definitely not the answer. I come from a family with a history of alcoholism, so drowning my workplace sorrows in a buttery chardonnay was not going to be the best response for me. Growing up with the Ad Council's "This is your brain on drugs..." burned egg message turned me off (and a whole generation, I'm afraid) to both fried eggs and recreational drugs, so painkillers were not an option for me either. Instead, I opted for chocolate and fast food.

I became a regular at the drive-thru of the fast-food joint which bears my name, and I super-sized everything. I'm ashamed to admit I knew most of the drive-thru menu by number.

But that wasn't all. I kept a stash of chocolate in my desk drawer, and each time I was asked to do something distasteful, I rewarded myself with a fistful of chocolate.

Several pounds and a cavity later, I can safely attest to you that "a spoonful of sugar" does not make the medicine go down or the toxic work environment go away.

If self-medication isn't the answer, then it must be self-esteem, right? After all, if you have awesome rock-solid self-esteem, you can get through anything just by knowing you're terrific inside and out.

Even Winnie-the-Pooh, A.A. Milne's portly little bear of yore, had that one down, saying, "Always remember, you're braver than you believe, stronger than you seem, and smarter than you think."

But when you're in a situation with office bullies and mean-girls, it's easy to forget that you're all that and a bag of chips, too, and you can find you've slipped from wearing your mortarboard and silky tassels at graduation and feeling like the queen of the mountain to understanding what it's like to be a doormat – face down with the word, WELCOME emblazoned across your body.

Drama & Door Slams?

There are a couple of things to think about before you take the long walk down the hall and slam that toxic workplace door behind you. First, visualize that walk a million times if you'd like; I think that's actually helpful.

But when you visualize it, remember that most doors don't slam effectively anymore, so the final staccato slam you're dreaming of will probably end up looking and sounding very awkward and lame because you'll have your arms loaded with all of your personal items tossed into a copy paper box with no lid (what happens to all the lids from those boxes, anyway?), and the door is probably not designed to slam anyway. "Whoosh, click," is not nearly as effective as a good old-fashioned soap opera door slam.

Confrontation?

Whether you're great at confrontation or not, a toxic workplace is often not the best place to test your confrontational skills, especially if you're new in the workforce or haven't found your solid footing yet. It's also hard to jump into being confrontation when you really need the job to keep a roof over your head or feed your family.

If you find yourself in a situation like the one I was in, before you give yourself high blood pressure, drink yourself into oblivion, or find something else to numb your pain, refer back to that JPM tattoo I mentioned earlier. There is some temporary motivation in knowing there will be a paycheck at the end of the week, and this kind of treatment inspires you to do some serious exploring for what human resource officers politely refer to as a "better fit."

Choosing Your Battles

If you are biting your lip until it bleeds to keep you from giving a much-needed piece of your mind to your toxic supervisor or boss, you might want to ask yourself, "Is this the hill I want to die on?"

Though there are many theories on where this phrase originally came from, most of them are military in nature, and nearly all of them are a way of asking you to consider how important this one battle is in the grand scheme of your life? Sometimes I think that's a great question to ask yourself, and during times of exceptional stress in a work situation, I often put a sticky note on my laptop or office wall to remind me that it may not be.

Of course, there are times when the answer to the question, "Is this the hill I want to die on?" will be a resounding, "Damned right it is!" and if that's the case – then you must listen to your gut. For me, it wasn't the toxic co-workers or the unrelenting assault of bullying and humiliation they incurred that took me to the edge.

When I finally realized that they were merely the big fish in that particular pond, I just started quietly looking for another pond. I'm not sure why they were surprised when I found it, but I knew they'd find someone else to turn into their workplace doormat.

However, in another position, I was asked to falsify records that would have made the organization look more favorable in a pending legal case involving children. When I asked myself, "Is this the hill I want to die on?" it didn't take long for the answer to come. My inner voice practically stomped up and down in my psyche and screamed, "Well, duh! Someone is asking you to lie because she didn't do her job and put others in jeopardy? If this isn't the hill you'll die on, then what is?" I quickly found a new position in another company.

Listen to Your Gut

Author John Powell once said, "When I repress my emotions, my stomach keeps score." He was right, and while it's true that what doesn't kill you makes you stronger, it's also true that if you swallow a lot of poison, you'll get sick or possibly die.

If you're experiencing a toxic workplace, you have a choice. You can either try to make it better, or you can find the fire exit and get the heck out of the burning building because there's a good chance it's not going to get better until you do. Like a toxic or abusive relationship, you may love the abuser (or the job), but that doesn't mean you should stay in the relationship.

If you want to find your happily ever after, find your courage and start looking for a place to work that doesn't ask you to give up yourself, your integrity, or your dignity.

Chapter 3 Nuggets

- Chocolate, wine, donuts, and prescription pain pills are temporary except for the weight gain, hangovers, ulcers, and constipation, that is. If you're in a toxic work situation, self-medication is not the answer. Neither is becoming a doormat or losing your dignity.

- You may be the most confident person in the world, but workplace bullies are everywhere, and they have a knack for chipping away at your self-confidence and energy. Know that, and don't let them get the best of you. If you can't confront the workplace toxins (and I get it, sometimes you simply can't), start looking for the emergency exits, and get out before you're asked to compromise your integrity or your dignity. Both are too important to give up.

- I wish like crazy I could tell you that you can fix a toxic work environment, but in my experience, the only thing that will fix it is a 'deep cleaning' that gets rid of nearly everyone. For me, I've found that as long as the place is still making a profit or the work is getting done every day, nobody in management wants to do more than a feather dusting of the visible shelves. Lots of toxic workplaces are toxic from the top down, and like the trickle-down theories of economics, it takes generations for change to occur. Know that the change may not happen while you're there, and find the lifeboats before the iceberg actually hits.

Chapter 4

How Can Working for a Micromanager Help Me?

We've all met micromanagers, and usually, we dislike them immediately and immensely. Mine was Mrs. North, whose name I have changed even though it was so long ago I hardly imagine she is still in this earthly plane of existence. If she is, no doubt she is still tormenting some poor, newbie convenience store clerk with her cloying micromanaging.

Mrs. North owned the convenience store I worked at for a few short months while I was in college. Her reason for hiring me was because she'd seen my work ethic and customer service skills in action when I worked for a nearby, rival convenience store she was spying on.

Every day when I clocked in, Mrs. North would walk me back into the cooler and explain to me how to rotate the dairy products by putting the newest cartons of milk at the back and sliding them forward, so the older ones would be purchased first. It was not rocket science. Despite having learned how to 'rotate stock' at my previous convenience store gig, which happened to be the kind that sold milk in glass bottles requiring the rotating stock, Mrs. North took the time to teach me this very important job detail each and every day. Even after she'd 'promoted' me to assistant manager, Mrs. North still made a point of reminding me every single day to rotate the stock.

And that wasn't the only menial task the poor woman couldn't let go of in her business. I must have been schooled in how to count change and keep the bills in the cash register facing the same direction at least a hundred times, too. To say that got old fast would be an understatement of epic proportions. I got out – fast.

Micromanagers can teach you so much about career and life; odd as it seems, it's really a gift to be exposed to one early in your career. From a micromanager, you'll learn how to prioritize work and life because a micromanager typically cannot accomplish this task. The micromanager will give you a task or responsibility that you start out being really excited about – like putting together a report or organizing a database or filing system.

And if the micromanager did that and then went away, you'd do a great job, feel valuable in your position, and probably put your very best effort into making sure the project was done beautifully. Unfortunately, a micromanager can't seem to get out of her own way, and she feeds on getting into yours.

Suddenly, instead of organizing the database or filing system alphabetically, your micromanager wants to teach you the Alphabet Song, usually with a chipper and helpful line like an aging cheerleader or hall monitor, saying, "Gee! I have an idea of how you can get this done super-fast by using this great song I learned when I was a little girl. Here, let me sing it for you."

Micromanagers are the perfect role model of what not to do or be when you are in a position of authority because they tend to relish whatever tiny little bit of power they've achieved or been granted and wield it like a passive-aggressive weapon against otherwise motivated employees and staff members.

The micromanager is the one who makes you realize how important a little trust and latitude are in the workplace. Sadly, no matter how well you do your job or the task at hand, the micromanager is absolutely positive that she could do it better. And it is my firm belief that many businesses would be farther ahead and far more profitable and proactive if the micromanagers could be reassigned to a role that does not involve systematically crushing the creativity and morale of staff.

If you have micromanaging tendencies (and I believe we all do in some areas), do more than your best to keep them in check. Once you've given an employee or volunteer a task, simply smile, bite your tongue to keep you from adding a helpful suggestion on how to accomplish that task, and walk the heck away.

The result may not be exactly what you wanted or expected, but it will be a result that allows your staff member to keep his or her dignity while also expressing a bit of individuality and creativity – two things you need in order to keep the company's mission current and vibrant.

Working for a micromanager will help you, not only by teaching you how not to act when you are in a position of power, but by providing a great role model of how to motivate employees to take ownership and begin to accept their job as a career, not just a job. Along the way, those empowered staff members will begin to share ideas that will help increase productivity and profitability, and they will be expending their efforts to help make the company a better place.

When an employee is happy and feels valued and listened to, she is more likely to want to maintain or even grow that good feeling.

Likewise, when an employee is reminded every day how to do the most menial of jobs or that someone else can always do it better, faster, more efficiently, or more beautifully, he quickly becomes disillusioned, feels devalued, and starts to resent being treated as though he is incapable of the manager's trust and respect.

If You Love Something, Set it Free

Back in the 1970's, we all had posters emblazoned with author Richard Bach's phrase, "If you love something, set it free." And that's as true in business and work relationships as it is in soulmates and the brilliant energy of white light and positive affirmations. Some of our posters went a little farther and finished the whole statement, which I believe was spoken by a bird learning about life in the insanely popular book and movie, *Jonathan Livingston Seagull*. "If you love something, set it free. If it returns to you, it's yours. If it doesn't, it never was."

Aside from begging the question of how a talking seagull became the spokes-bird for a generation in the 1970's, there is some real life-wisdom in knowing the importance of giving latitude if you want to earn trust and loyalty. Those managers who offer you latitude when assigning you a task or project are far more likely to earn your respect and make you want to work harder and more creatively to produce the best result possible.

The Mrs. Norths of your world simply make you want to take your talents elsewhere to keep you from the daily lesson in how to put the old milk at the front of the shelf where it will be picked up before the new stuff. Learn to seek out the managers who don't crush your soul, and learn to appreciate the latitude you are given, and before you know it, like Jonathan Livingston Seagull, you'll be sailing above the storms of life, free as a bird and finding perfection in creativity and work.

Chapter 4 Nuggets

- Always put the new milk at the back of the shelf and slide the older stuff to the front.

- You will run into micromanagers in life. How you deal with them will impact your career and your blood pressure. You can either make yourself sick fighting the micromanager or trying to get her to trust you or keep calm and call out your inner seagull. If you can learn to let it go and pity the micromanager's poor family (because can you imagine having to learn how to set the table or load the dishwasher every day of your life?), you'll survive and learn an important lesson about how not to manage others.

- Whether it's a paid or volunteer gig, a micromanager is one of the leading causes of turnover. A micromanager can help you to understand and appreciate the importance of latitude. None of us wants to be watched over like a hawk (again with the bird metaphors?), especially when we've been led to believe the task assigned is an important and valued responsibility. Once you've had a micromanager in your life, you'll appreciate and respect the good managers even more, and if you pay attention and learn from the micromanager, you'll be a better manager or supervisor of others at work and at home. Your kids may thank you for not helicopter parenting them, and you'll have to put far less money in the therapy jar you should start for them on the day they are born.

- Micromanagers prove to you that life is like the wisdom of a lone seagull named Jonathan. "If you love something, you must set it free."

Chapter 5

If I Know it's a Dead-End Job, Why Stay?

Life is short. You're right. Nobody ever said from his deathbed, "Golly, I wish I'd stayed in that crappy job and worked for those asshats a few months longer." You're right. "Tomorrow is never promised to us." You're right. You're right. You're right. And I know what you're thinking. You're thinking, "Life is short. If I'm in a crappy, dead-end job, why should I stay?" And you're right. Life is short, and it seems crazy and counterintuitive to stay in a crappy, dead-end job working for an asshat (or several).

And most of the time, you should get out of that crappy, dead-end job and rid yourself of the asshats. But sometimes you must put on your invisible nose plugs and stick around for a while, even if you know it's not where you're meant to be.

When you were a toddler, you never worried about time, and tomorrow only mattered on the days immediately preceding your birthday, a visit from Santa, and a visit to be spoiled by Grandma.

As a toddler, you sampled everything, stuck most of it in your greedy, little mouth, threw up once in a while, played all the time, and when you were exhausted, you crashed. Life was good, and you didn't spend your days fretting about tomorrow or thinking about your "long term goals," unless, of course long term meant the ice cream truck or trip to the park your mom promised you'd get after you got up from your afternoon nap.

So when did you start to get all weird and neurotic about time, winning, and being at the top of the food chain power-wise and financially?

While I'd love to blame it all on "reality" television shows like *Survivor®*, *The Apprentice®* and *Keeping Up with the Kardashians* for the current preoccupation with instant fame and fortune, it goes back a little farther. In fact, it's probably one of those things you can blame on your parents and grandparents.

After all, from the moment you were born, you were probably told you were above-average, maybe even exceptional in the areas of everything from physical appearance and intelligence to your proficiency in toilet training.

When you showed up for soccer practice at age four because your parents brought you there and cheered you on as you cried on the field and peed your pants (so much for that toilet training prowess), you were probably rewarded with a trophy for *Enthusiastic Participation, Best Smile, or Happiest Camper.*

And those accolades continued whether you deserved them or not. In an attempt to ensure that no child was left behind, every child was given the title of exceptional student, brightest light, or winningest winner.

Unfortunately, childhood doesn't last forever, and before you know it, the cap and gown you wore at your most recent graduation is stuffed in a corner at the back of your closet, and you're working any job you can find because you need to pay back those student loans and keep your car insurance current.

All those dreams you were encouraged to dream and all those pretty pictures on you're *The Secret* vision board seem pretty far out of reach when you're the low guy on the totem pole, or you're cleaning the bathrooms at the 24-hour restaurant everyone throws up in after a night of clubbing. If you catch a glimpse of yourself in the mirror, you might groan and ask yourself, "Isn't life too short for this?"

Life is Short, But it's Not Free

Yes, and no. Here's the thing. Life is short, but unless you were born a child of Prince William and Princess Kate, one of the Pitt-Jolie brood, or a spawn of the Trump dynasty, you're probably not going to start as the CEO of a multi-million-dollar corporation. And if you do, I think you'll be sorry. Life is short, but you still have to put in your time and pay some dues before you earn the respect and authority you have always been told you so rightly deserve.

Adam Liepzig, the CEO of Entertainment Media Partners, shared once that at his 25th college reunion at Yale, he was shocked to learn that eighty percent of his successful, wealthy, and gifted classmates were not happy with their lives, despite their meteoric careers, glittering lifestyles, and financial comfort. While they had graduated and reached all of their life's goals early on, many of them were simply not happy. That unhappiness and discontent in our lives often stems from things coming a bit too easily for us, and like a kid given free rein in a candy store, being given everything we want doesn't make us happy; often it makes us miserable.

And so it is with your career. It might seem wonderful to be handed the keys to a successful business or organization days after stuffing the cap and gown into the back of the closet, but we all need a little time to learn the ropes, test the waters, and figure out our leadership style and persona.

After all, you didn't hop on a bicycle and race off happily into the sunset, did you? More than likely, you had a set of training wheels, and when you and your family finally decided to remove them, you had the luxury of someone huffing and puffing as they ran along beside you, helping you balance as you begged them not to let go.

Maybe you still remember the feeling of exhilaration and accomplishment when you finally realized that no one was running along beside you, holding on as you pedaled feverishly.

If you do remember, even if it's a hazy memory, then you probably have a good idea of what it will feel like when you know you're ready to cut loose from the dead-end job because you've paid your dues, learned from the asshats, and collected a few assets of your own to be used as you move on to the next adventure.

Vision and Vomit

Yes, life is short, but it's also a process which requires learning, practice, and even falling down a few times. The same is true for your career, and as hard as it may seem to have to live through the struggle and endure a few asshats along the way, that is an important part of the process.

In my first waitressing gig, I worked for a 24-hour restaurant chain that was doomed from the start because of its tremendously racist name. I wore a burnt sienna polyester uniform that always smelled like old grease (we all did), and I always seemed to get scheduled with a waitress who was sleeping with the sleazy manager of the restaurant.

When she wasn't in back, slacking off on her customers to enjoy a little private time with the boss, she was trying to steal the tips from my tables and making sure I always had the task of cleaning the bathrooms after a bar rush.

Every morning as I drove home bleary-eyed, stinking of old grease and the super strength cleaner used to handle drunken vomit, I rededicated myself to getting out of the job as soon as I could. I'd count my tips (drunk people usually do tip pretty well, even if it isn't always intentional), pay for my groceries with quarters and tip change, and plan for my future.

I am a clumsy fool, and I knew from the first time I donned that nasty, polyester uniform that I wasn't cut out to be a waitress, but I forced myself to stay in the job for a few months, saved the money and lived frugally, and did a whole lot of observing and learning about how to treat people.

Waitressing may have been something I did because I needed money, but it gave me a chance to learn that you can make great career connections anywhere and impress them mightily – even over a side of hash browns.

I also learned the importance of remembering what was important to my customers – knowing how they took their coffee or how they liked their toast meant a better tip and a bit of respect.

And observing first hand that nepotism (sleeping with the boss) didn't really get you a whole lot further ahead (they broke up, so she got fired; he stole from the company, so he got fired) was an important thing to learn and kept me from having to make that same mistake myself in other, more meaningful jobs during the course of my career.

Yes, it is true that life is short. It is also statistically true that you are not likely to get hit by a truck tomorrow, so you don't need to rush and race with time because you must be a winner the very minute the shot is fired and the race starts.

Not every job is going to be good; in fact, there will be a few dead-end jobs in your career history, and that's okay.

Actually, it's more than okay because the dead-end jobs are a great place to learn what your style is, make mistakes without branding yourself forever, and add skills to your skillset and connections to your toolbox to help you get interviews and references for later on when you are ready to start your real-life and real-life-career.

Most importantly, those dead-end jobs – even waitressing, will help teach you to be kind to everyone – even the drunks during bar rush – because you never know who's going to stagger through the door drunk today, and come back tomorrow, hungover but with a memory of the nice waitress who helped clean up and fed you toast after you trashed the public restroom in a drunken stupor the night before.

Sure, you could have treated that drunken slob the way he deserved to be treated given his condition, but your composure, kindness, and understanding are a lot more positive a memory than a bitter woman in dirty polyester who slings your meal at you and slops the coffee with a dour face.

Chapter 5 Nuggets

- Life is short. Not only does this mean you have my permission to eat dessert first, but it also means that you shouldn't stay in a dead-end, crappy job for your whole life just because there's a paycheck. Along with that paycheck will eventually come ulcers, addiction, and misery. But don't jump ship the first time you have a bad day, either.

- You're not going to start as CEO, and you probably won't ever be famous enough to be referred to by one name only (ala Beyoncé or Madonna), but you wouldn't really be happy if you did, so enjoy the ascent and learn as much as you can on the way.

- You're probably not going to get hit by a truck tomorrow, and while it's important to remember that life is short, don't get so caught up in chasing the brass ring or imagining your own untimely demise that you forget to enjoy the moment you're in right now. Remember the tortoise and the hare and the moral of the story that, "Slow and steady wins the race"? Well, that's not the worst moral to follow, as long as you remember to stop and smell the flowers along the way. You'll still beat that cocky hare in the end, and you'll have been able to do it without prescription drugs, steroids, or crazy mood swings.

- When carrying coffee or hot liquids, don't look at the liquid sloshing around in the vessel. This one simple tip will keep you from spilling gallons of hot liquid onto your already gross polyester uniform. Additional nugget – I'm pretty sure when hot liquid comes into contact with polyester, it causes skin to melt, and it hurts a lot.

- I hope you never have to do this – really, but if you want to live through cleaning up vomit (especially someone else's drunken vomit), baking soda or corn starch are good to have handy. I also recommend a seriously good broom and dustpan that you won't mind washing, rubber gloves, and a shit ton of paper towels (yes, I am quite sure that's the official quantity necessary to do the job).

Chapter 6

How Do I Handle Shit Jobs on My Resumé

and in Interviews?

Being fired or laid off sucks, but it happens to the best of us. Sometimes it happens because you have a lesson to learn about practicing professionalism, playing well with others, or having a good work ethic, and other times it happens because you have more integrity than your employer. That especially sucks because you're doing the right thing, being honest, and still getting thrown under the bus and out the door.

If this has happened to you, I'm sorry because it's like an earthquake to your self-esteem. If you've been axed for being honest and not selling out for the paycheck that we both know you need really badly, good for you!

I think it was author C.S. Lewis who said, "Integrity is doing the right thing even when no one is watching."

If the truth is that you screwed up, then please do yourself a favor and take responsibility for it. Adlai Stevenson, an incredible American statesman, once said, "It is often easier to fight for one's principles than to live up to them."

That sounds like something a two-time candidate for the Presidency of the United States would say, but in Stevenson's case, he came by that wisdom the hard way. He screwed up big-time when he was just twelve years old, and it cost a sixteen year-old girl named Ruth Merwin her life.

It happened at a party – a venue where teens historically try to impress one another. Stevenson had fetched a gun for an older boy – a student in military school.

The older boy checked the gun meticulously to be sure it was not loaded and showed off his recently-learned arms skills. When he handed the gun back to the twelve year-old Stevenson, the gun discharged, hitting Merwin in the forehead and killing her instantly.

Though Stevenson never faced charges and was completely exonerated, he carried the burden of his actions throughout his life, rarely speaking of it, but becoming known for his genuine humility, his self-deprecating personality, and his passion for peace.

The reason I bring up Stevenson and his assertion that it is often easier to fight for one's principles than to live up to them is because if you lost your job because you screwed up, own it. Accept the blame, examine why you made that decision (or failed to make the right ones), and learn from it. Then move on. Don't beat yourself up. Don't blame your parents, your professors, your lover, or the rest of the world – just learn from it and move on.

"I Cannot Tell a Lie…"

But what happens when you score a job interview and the question of that gap in your résumé or the inevitable, "Why did you leave your previous position?" question comes up? Do you reach deep and get in touch with your inner George Washington and 'fess up about the old cherry tree, or do you dazzle them with your B.S. fluency?

The answer is simple and makes me think of my grandmother, God rest her soul, who said, "Oh what a tangled web we weave, when first we practice to deceive." Okay, so maybe Sir Walter Scott said it before my grandma, but he never slipped me a dollar and told me to go buy myself a grape soda, so I'm giving this one to my grandma.

The thing is, you need to tell the truth because it is probably going to come out eventually anyway. A few years ago, a great friend lost his fabulous, six-figure job because the company he worked for found out that, while he'd been doing the job brilliantly for more than twenty years, he really didn't have a college degree.

He'd lied about it on his resumé, and all those years later, all the success he'd had didn't amount to a thing against the one lie he'd told in desperation to land a job in order to feed his young family. It will be the same thing with you, even if you are a really good prevaricator.

If you've got to tell a particularly unpleasant detail about your job history, do it with honesty, humility, and the sage wisdom of what you learned. If you got caught stealing boxes of pens from the company stockroom and were unceremoniously fired, explain to the interviewer that you were young, starving, and made a really stupid decision that you instantly regretted.

You can explain that you have sought help, spoken with a therapist, joined a twelve-step group, and though you are not proud of this unseemly part of your history, it is yours and you feel you have become a better, stronger, and wiser person because of the error and poor decision-making skills of your youth.

I wish I could tell you that this will always get you off the hook and allow your incredibly wise potential employer to see what a gem you are now that you've been polished up a bit and are grinding off some of the rough edges of youth, but the truth is this – sometimes it works, and sometimes it doesn't.

When it doesn't, or when the potential employer rushes to end the interview, and your gut tells you honesty may not have been the best policy after all, you're wrong.

Honesty is always the best policy, and if the company can't see past your youthful indiscretion or the mistake to which you have humbly confessed to this prominent stranger, you wouldn't have enjoyed working there anyway. Trust that, and move on. I promise, it's better than lying.

Should You Out the Asshats?

And what if you left your last job unwillingly because you worked for a complete asshat who was a living example of the Peter Principle (Google it; you're going to totally appreciate this!)? Should you talk about your former employer with the same honesty we just discussed when it came to being fired for doing something uber-stupid? Sorry, wrong number. Here's the thing: that potential boss sitting across the table interviewing you is going to one day be a former employer, too.

So while you're there regaling the tremendously rapt audience of one, two, or a full committee of interviewers about how stupid your last supervisor was, what is going through the mind of your interviewer is this, "Wow! If he's speaking this way about his last employer, what do you think he'll say about me and our company if he leaves on less than amicable terms? I mean, he tells a great story, but I wonder if he's the real asshat in this scenario?

If you talk shit about your former employer, you'd better be prepared to eat some of the smelly, gross stuff yourself.

Know it, and even if the last job was the nightmare job from Hell, find a less explosive way to share that the former position was simply not a good fit for your personality, work style, or career goals.

Another friend worked for an independent crop research farm which was charged with performing pesticide trials on vegetables in a variety of conditions. When one of the scientists erroneously dumped a hundred times the pesticide chemicals on the test crop, the company didn't want to lose the client, its money, or the perfect record it boasted in all its ads and proposals.

The owners insisted on altering the records and results, which could have changed the pesticide company's application instructions once on the market or worse – could have led to dangerous chemical levels for any individual who consumed test vegetables.

My friend left the job rather than participate in the unethical scheme, but it was difficult to find work in the same field without ratting out his former employer to his potential new employers – all of whom were competitors.

Meanwhile, his former employers began a pretty hearty smear campaign against their former employee, for while he had acted with integrity, they were petrified that he might blow the whistle on them. They went to great lengths to denigrate the honest man's integrity, making it hard for him to find work in the field – for about a year.

And while I'm not entirely sure about karma, I do know that my friend's phone started ringing with offers when his former employer's business closed under a cloud of suspicion over the validity of its most recent trials. My friend didn't say a bad word about his previous employer; he just continued to live an honest life with no thought of revenge or malice. The company was responsible for its own demise.

Should You Confess Everything on the First Date?

With all this talk of honesty and integrity, you might think you have to tell all of your secrets and reveal every single one of your flaws in the first interview. Please don't. I'm not asking you to be oblique or phony, but let's think this through using a couple of fun facts I alluded to in an earlier chapter.

Did you know that, according to a study from Microsoft Corporation, the average attention span of a goldfish is nine seconds. Once you finish thinking about how exactly Microsoft executed that study and how much money it cost to learn this fact about the lowly goldfish, you'll be interested to learn that the study also found that, since the turn of the century, the average attention span of a human being dropped from twelve seconds to eight seconds.

What that means is that you have approximately seven seconds to make a first impression on someone, so it might be better to spend those first seven seconds making a good impression instead of launching into the preamble to your personal confession. Instead of sharing that you sucked your thumb until you were a freshman in college, that you still like to lick the frosting out of the center of the Oreo® before eating the crunchy outside, or that you aren't exactly the most punctual person ever to punch a time clock, it might be better to show your best side and save a little of the mystery until after you've nailed the first interview.

A widower friend who was married for decades tells the story of courting his late wife. He fell in love with her the first time he saw her. She was perfect, and when he decided to pop the question, he made sure it was a romantic setting and that everything was perfect because they were in love, and he was sure she'd accept his proposal with much joy.

To his surprise, when he proposed, she began to cry and between sobs, apologetically declined. Shell shocked and speechless, he instinctively took her into his arms to comfort her.

When she was finally able to speak through her tears, she explained that she was a Type I diabetic, and she was not expected to live much past her twentieth birthday, and she was certainly never going to be able to give her beloved the children she knew he wanted. She had been afraid to tell him because she loved him so deeply and was sure he wouldn't want to waste his time and love on such a high-risk bride.

I attended her funeral services just a few months ago – only weeks before what would have been the couple's 49th wedding anniversary. My friend swears he would have married his beloved even if she'd told him at their first meeting of her illness, but it's easy to believe that long after that first, wonderful impression had been made.

We've all been on dreadful first dates, blind dates, or worst of all, dates with someone who recently broke up with a longtime love. Usually, those evenings are long and scream for anesthesia as we sit listening politely to someone tell their entire, unabridged and very sad story of love and loss, bonding and betrayal. We usually end the evening with a pitiful smile, knowing that we'll never see one another again because we don't know one another well, yet we know way too many intimate details of each other's tragic experience with relationship. Just like in love, I think it's best to not share everything on the first date or in the first job interview. With any luck, almost 49 years from now you can thank me for that advice.

Chapter 6 Nuggets

- Honesty really is the best policy. I know it's not sexy or alluring, and I know it's something your parents have told you since the first time you pointed a finger at your sibling to get yourself off the hook. Sexy or not, it's true. Not only will it help you sleep better, it's simply the right thing to do.

- Don't talk shit unless you are prepared to eat some. If you're going to say horrible things about your former employer, even if they are all absolutely true and it feels so very good to do, know that you may have entertained the audience (your interviewers), but you've very probably lost the job. That might feel okay for a few minutes, but when your rent is due and you don't have a job, the vengeful glow of that moment won't feel

The letters were answered by a psychologist who
med to try really hard to make the marriage work
pite what seemed like insurmountable issues of
st, infidelity, financial woes, and parenting problems.
n, the written answer asked the troubled housewife
'd written (and all of us eavesdropping on her pitiful
the typical open-ended questions like, "How does
make you feel?"

I miss Betsy McCall, and I've long-replaced my
This Marriage Be Saved? addiction for a high spot
e *Ask Amy* advice columnist fan club. You should
right out and buy her books, write wonderful
vs, and tell her I sent you. Some of that advice has
with me when I've been in those 'rock and hard
spots where I didn't think I'd last another day
g for the asshat boss or toxic workplace. So how
know when it's time to start quietly packing up
opier box of desktop frames and Dilbert® cartoons
aft your resignation letter?

quite as warm as it did when you were in the
spotlight during the interview.

- I know I said to be honest in everything, but that
  does not mean you have to admit to your potential
  employer that you suffer from debilitating
  menstrual cramps, refuse to be on the same
  planet as a carnivore, or have an affinity for
  Sunday morning mimosas and bacon. There are
  some things you may want to save until after
  you've been on the job for a while. If asked
  specifically if you engage in key parties (look it up
  in your Urban Dictionary) with your condo
  association, you should probably plead the Fifth
  and consider not accepting the job even if it's
  offered, (that is, after all, a pretty illegal interview
  question), but other than that, I think you serve
  yourself best if you are always honest.

- What goes around comes back around, life is a
  circle, karma is a bitch – use whatever platitude

you want – they're all true. As fluffy and New Age-y as it sounds, there is something to be said for the law of attraction, and there is proof that what you put out into the mighty Universe is typically what you get back. If you put out good stuff and live an honest life, you're much more likely to have those good energies coming back in your direction. If you hang out with a bunch of thugs, you're probably going to be pulled over by law enforcement more often. If you don't say bad things about other people (even asshat former bosses or co-workers), they're not likely to trash you, either.

- Keep calm and stay true. Honesty really is the best policy.

- Have you Googled "Peter Principle" yet? Go ahead. I'll wait.

Chapter 7

When is it Time to Throw in the To[w]

When I was a child, I used to lov[e] grandmother's McCall's magazines. Eve[ry] were new fashions I could cut out a[nd] Betsy McCall paper doll in the magazin[e] sick of making Betsy look like a super[m] the exciting adventures in her life, s[o] the grown-up features in the magazine[s]

One particular favorite was the [] *Be Saved?* section, where lonely hous[e] their souls and share stories of mar[r] their spark, relationships filled with [] frustration, and spite.

Throwing the towel in on a toxic workplace can sometimes be the only answer, but as mentioned earlier, be sure you think it through before you walk out the door, never to return. Ask yourself the workplace version of the "Can this marriage be saved?" question, and then sleep on it and ask yourself again.

The answer may still be, "Absolutely not!" but it's important that you know you have given the matter serious consideration because someone (usually a parent or passive aggressive frenemy) will make you wonder if maybe you weren't a bit hasty in your decision. If you think it through, you'll be able to repel their type of toxic love with your own pragmatism and conscientious pre-consideration.

If You Leave, Learn

Leaving a toxic workplace is sometimes the only answer to preserve your sanity and your career. If you feel that staying in the toxic work situation is going to turn you into a toxic person too, then by all means, digest the lessons you've learned there and get the heck out while you can.

You don't want to become what's sometimes known as a straw boss, which is kind of an assistant to a boss or supervisor who is charged with supervising and motivating (often cruelly) the work of a small group of workers.

If you pick up the attitude of the asshats in your workplace, you're very likely doomed to become a perpetual assistant asshat yourself, and I'll bet you we've all experienced a couple of those folks and don't ever want to emulate them.

When you know it's time to make your exit, know that you're not the first one to leave a toxic situation. There are loads of examples of exiting a toxic relationship, whether it's a marriage or spouse-equivalent you need to distance yourself from in order to stay safe and be able to move forward emotionally or a relationship of Biblical proportions.

After all, even Jesus, historically known as the only perfect and flaw-free human being since the world began, only lasted three years in a super-toxic work environment, and you and I definitely don't have the same happy ending opportunity he had.

Even though it may have been a job you loved when you got it and had high hopes for retiring from, when it's time to go, you usually know it. And once you've made the decision, the days until you execute your plan can seem to take an eternity, can't they? You might ask yourself if it would just be easier and more efficient to just go for the dramatic exit?

The short answer is simple – no, but the reasons for the short answer are not as simple. I humbly suggest that, even for the crappiest job, take a little time, write out a positive resignation letter, and provide at least two weeks' notice to your employer.

If you're lucky, this strategy will net you a good recommendation from your current 'bosshole' or colleagues, make you look a lot better to your next employer, and free you from any guilt or regret over how you left. It's also the most decent thing you can do for your workmates and colleagues, most of whom will be sticking around and will be forced to pick up the slack and your responsibilities once you're gone.

quite as warm as it did when you were in the spotlight during the interview.

- I know I said to be honest in everything, but that does not mean you have to admit to your potential employer that you suffer from debilitating menstrual cramps, refuse to be on the same planet as a carnivore, or have an affinity for Sunday morning mimosas and bacon. There are some things you may want to save until after you've been on the job for a while. If asked specifically if you engage in key parties (look it up in your Urban Dictionary) with your condo association, you should probably plead the Fifth and consider not accepting the job even if it's offered, (that is, after all, a pretty illegal interview question), but other than that, I think you serve yourself best if you are always honest.

- What goes around comes back around, life is a circle, karma is a bitch – use whatever platitude you want – they're all true. As fluffy and New Age-y as it sounds, there is something to be said for the law of attraction, and there is proof that what you put out into the mighty Universe is typically what you get back. If you put out good stuff and live an honest life, you're much more likely to have those good energies coming back in your direction. If you hang out with a bunch of thugs, you're probably going to be pulled over by law enforcement more often. If you don't say bad things about other people (even asshat former bosses or co-workers), they're not likely to trash you, either.

- Keep calm and stay true. Honesty really is the best policy.

- Have you Googled "Peter Principle" yet? Go ahead. I'll wait.

Chapter 7

When is it Time to Throw in the Towel and Quit?

When I was a child, I used to love looking at my grandmother's McCall's magazines. Every month, there were new fashions I could cut out and place on the Betsy McCall paper doll in the magazine, and when I got sick of making Betsy look like a supermodel dressed for the exciting adventures in her life, sometimes I'd read the grown-up features in the magazine.

One particular favorite was the *Can This Marriage Be Saved?* section, where lonely housewives would bare their souls and share stories of marriages that had lost their spark, relationships filled with rejection, dejection, frustration, and spite.

The letters were answered by a psychologist who seemed to try really hard to make the marriage work despite what seemed like insurmountable issues of trust, infidelity, financial woes, and parenting problems. Often, the written answer asked the troubled housewife who'd written (and all of us eavesdropping on her pitiful life) the typical open-ended questions like, "How does that make you feel?"

I miss Betsy McCall, and I've long-replaced my *Can This Marriage Be Saved?* addiction for a high spot in the *Ask Amy* advice columnist fan club. You should rush right out and buy her books, write wonderful reviews, and tell her I sent you. Some of that advice has stuck with me when I've been in those 'rock and hard place' spots where I didn't think I'd last another day working for the asshat boss or toxic workplace. So how do you know when it's time to start quietly packing up your copier box of desktop frames and Dilbert® cartoons and draft your resignation letter?

Throwing the towel in on a toxic workplace can sometimes be the only answer, but as mentioned earlier, be sure you think it through before you walk out the door, never to return. Ask yourself the workplace version of the "Can this marriage be saved?" question, and then sleep on it and ask yourself again.

The answer may still be, "Absolutely not!" but it's important that you know you have given the matter serious consideration because someone (usually a parent or passive aggressive frenemy) will make you wonder if maybe you weren't a bit hasty in your decision. If you think it through, you'll be able to repel their type of toxic love with your own pragmatism and conscientious pre-consideration.

If You Leave, Learn

Leaving a toxic workplace is sometimes the only answer to preserve your sanity and your career. If you feel that staying in the toxic work situation is going to turn you into a toxic person too, then by all means, digest the lessons you've learned there and get the heck out while you can.

You don't want to become what's sometimes known as a straw boss, which is kind of an assistant to a boss or supervisor who is charged with supervising and motivating (often cruelly) the work of a small group of workers.

If you pick up the attitude of the asshats in your workplace, you're very likely doomed to become a perpetual assistant asshat yourself, and I'll bet you we've all experienced a couple of those folks and don't ever want to emulate them.

Be Gracious, and Don't Gossip

Once you've made the decision, even though the time until you leave will seem like forever, try not to call in sick, use up all your vacation and personal days, or gloat to your colleagues by ceremoniously counting down the days, hours, and minutes until you're liberated. It will be hard, but please refrain from doing the happy dance every time you clock out or singing, "Three more days to go...." each time you bump into an associate at the water cooler. Show a little class – yes, you have some, thank you, and take the high road. It may not give you the same instant gratification as flipping off everyone who has ever underestimated you, but it will make you a better person and leave less of a bitter taste in you and the mouth of others when you leave.

Don't spend your lunch breaks talking about what jerks you work for and how glad you'll be to get rid of them. Resist the urge (and it will be a strong urge) to join the crew of Debbie Downers (and every workplace has them) in trashing the place, and don't use your last days on the job to thumb your nose or shoot a moon at everyone who has wronged you. You are better than that, and besides, you'll be gone soon.

Why continue to eat poison and hope your opponents are the ones who die from it? You've made a decision to change and move forward; don't take three steps back in the process. If you do, you are likely to end up in the same place six months from now in your new job, wondering how you keep landing in these toxic work situations when the real problem may be the same face that scowls back at you in the mirror every morning.

I'm not trying to be Little Mary Sunshine here; I'm just hoping you'll realize that you're far too good and valuable to stoop to petty gossip, coffee klatch kvetching, and under-your-breath mumbling because you've already thought it through seriously, considered your options honestly and realistically, and made the decision to move ahead towards your goal of a happy life both in and out of the workplace. Once you've made that decision, applaud yourself and don't let the haters or the jealous losers get to you. They'll have plenty of time to talk about you when you're gone – and they will. And just as it happens with a former lover, you'll have plenty of time to journal about your former job and how grateful you are to have left it behind and learned from it when you've put a little distance between you.

Chapter 7 Nuggets

- You'll know when it's time to throw the towel in and start the process of leaving. Do think it through pragmatically and rationally, and don't rush to make the decision. I know you hate to have someone tell you to, "Sleep on it," before you make a final decision, but you should do just that. And then take a walk with your dog, spend a couple of hours riding your bike, hiking a waterfall, or meditating before you finalize that decision.

- Even Jesus only lasted three years in a toxic work environment, and He was perfect!

- Don't go for the dramatic exit; don't gloat, don't bad mouth your soon-to-be-former colleagues or workplace, and don't do the happy dance every time you remember that your time there is winding down. Take the high road.

- Jobs and relationships have something important in common. Both take a lot of work, and both have ups and downs. Be sure this isn't just one of those low spots before you call it a day and submit your resignation letter. When you stop loving what you do and start dreading getting up on the morning, it's probably time to either double-down and put in extra work on your job or relationship or start the process of letting go.

Chapter 8

Should I Burn the Damned Bridge?

A couple of years ago, an acquaintance left her position at a large company. She had been in a pretty comfortable spot, had worked there for many years, and had enjoyed great benefits, a good salary, and so much vacation time that mere mortals like you and I would unconsciously begin to drool just thinking about it. But she had what writer and tremendous motivational speaker Fawn Germer refers to as a 'bosshole,' and she felt she needed to get out before she had a breakdown.

She found a new job that would challenge her creativity, offer her the latitude she needed, and give her a chance to really shine. It was perfect. But when it came time for her exit interview, she decided it was her big chance to let the people in Human Resources know exactly what a bosshole her bosshole was.

She didn't hold back a bit, giving them both barrels of all the stupid mistakes the company had made and why she was choosing to leave them at the height of a successful career, which had also been very profitable for the company, too.

She let it all hang out, and when she left the exit interview, she really felt great. After all, she hadn't held anything back, and she'd let them know all their faults and mistakes. In short, she didn't just take a match to the bridge - she burned that sucker down to the ashy ground.

Unfortunately, while she felt great after letting all of the poison out of her system in the exit interview, all of the things she said in the exit interview made their way back to the very people she'd criticized and pointed fingers at during the interview.

One of the big bossholes she'd eviscerated happened to be very close to the corporate gift manager of one of the biggest donor corporations in the area. And while the contents of the exit interview should remain as private as the Catholic confessional booth, it doesn't always happen that way in real life.

Before she'd even sliced the Welcome Aboard cake at her new job in the nonprofit world, her organization had suddenly and unceremoniously lost one of its largest donors with no explanation. No, it doesn't seem fair, and it isn't exactly the highest bar of ethical behavior either, but it didn't have to be.

If the large corporation chose to offer an explanation at all, it simply needed to say that it had chosen to share its resources elsewhere that particular year (and evermore). And while my friend's new employers didn't have a clue why they'd suddenly lost one of their biggest donors, my friend did. Was it worth it to get her frustration off her chest?

I don't think so. Even though it made her feel great at the time, I think the guilt of knowing that her lambasting of her former employer had cost her new employer tens of thousands of dollars each year in support took away any of the warm feeling of revenge she may have experienced.

When you're finally ready to leave that less than stellar position, should you load up and have your list ready to let them know in explicit detail all their sins? Can you almost feel the angel on one shoulder and the devil on the other, battling it out to convince you to either take the high road or dive deep into the gutter? Should you burn the damned bridge?

No. No. No.

The answer is an emphatic no. No. No. No. And while I can unequivocally tell you that this is something you should not do, I can also tell you that it is not an easy thing to avoid.

As a woman with a whole lot of Irish in my DNA, I can tell you that what they say about the curse of the Irish is true. The curse of the Irish is said to be that we have long memories and short tempers.

To bite my tongue and clip out a pleasantry when I am feeling wronged, devalued, or disenfranchised seems to go against nearly every cell of my body. I can feel my blood starting to pump harder and my cheeks reddening in a betrayal of the calm and peaceful persona I am trying so hard to maintain.

What I'm saying is that I may not be the best teacher of this particular workplace skill, and if I can leave you with any bit of wisdom on this particular topic, it would surely be to, "Do as I say, not as I do." I try really hard to be unflappable and cool, but grace has never been my strong suit, and more often than not, I do almost anything I can to avoid the exit interview just to keep myself from unloading on some poor, unsuspecting human resource manager.

What seems like a lifetime ago, I worked as the administrative assistant (the term 'secretary' was on the exit ramp to extinction, and the place where I worked was uber-forward-thinking) in a personnel office (which is what they called Human Resource offices before they coined the name Human Resource offices).

Time and again I watched the Employment Specialist come out of exit interviews looking like she'd just been in a barroom brawl. Her ears were red, top lip pulled tight across her face in a forced smile that look more like a pissed off grimace, and her shoulders almost touching her earlobes from the stress she was carrying.

Sometimes, I'd be able to convince her to walk to the coffee shop, where she would invariably share the smallest of details of the exit interview she'd just completed.

And while she never shared trade secrets, it was clear to me that she had gotten more than an earful of everything the institution had done wrong and every sleight the exiting employee had ever felt he or she had incurred.

And while I know she had handled the exiting employee with more grace and dignity than I ever could have done, I know that her stomach was keeping score, and I'm not entirely sure any of the folks who had unburdened themselves during their exit interviews ever found long-term peace or happiness because they'd let it all hang out and "Let 'em have it."

When it's time to leave, if you've been reading and absorbing anything we've discussed so far, you already have a plan. You already know that whatever you say is not going to change the past, and it's probably not going to change the course of history either. If it does cause some tectonic plate shift in the company's atmosphere, what do you care?

After all, you'll be gone. Why waste all that good information on a company didn't know how to appreciate your amazing skill and talent when it had the chance? As Disney's Elsa would sing, "Let it go. Let it go!"

You've given them your time; you've shared your talent, and you've realized that they're not going to appreciate what you have to offer. Don't bother with the long and dramatic farewell scene. Just saunter off into the sunset as the credits roll and walk with your head held high.

Chances are good they'll be watching you walk out the door, seeing your confidence and calm, and wondering if they've just made a monumental mistake by letting you leave. Just keep walking, confident in the knowledge that yes, they have made a mistake by letting you go. But keep moving forward anyway because the best for you is yet to come.

Chapter 8 Nuggets

- Should you burn the damned bridge? No. No. And no. You're better than that. You're smarter than that, and you're stronger than that.

- An exit interview is the time to check and make sure you're getting all of your final reimbursements, including vacation and personal time you may be due. It's not the time to let them know that they should really fire your crappy bosshole, take a course in management skills, and change the brand of coffee in the coffee machine. Sure, that's what you want to say, and you can say that to your spouse, BFF, or even your ride or die circle over omelets at the 24-hour restaurant after you celebrate your last day in that hell hole where you used to work. (Just please, tip your waitress well – especially if you vomit hash browns.)

- Let it go. You are better than that, and to quote a Disney princess, "The cold never bothered me anyway." (If you now find that this song is stuck in your head all day, you're welcome.)

- Hold your head up high, and walk out the door with confidence a smile, and without looking back. You've got this.

Epilogue

Congratulations. You just finished a crash course in how to turn that crappy job into something you can take with you into the next chapter of your own career and personal life. If you're in a crummy job now or working for a major league asshat or bosshole, please know that you have my empathy because I know it's not where you really want to be. Also know that I commend you for not just pulling the covers over your head and giving up.

The fact that you've gotten this far says a lot about you; not the least of which is that you're motivated and ready to make lemonade out of those lemons life may have handed you recently.

So where should you go from here? Wherever you want. Whether you are ready to admit it or not, you're the one in the driver's seat, and the decision to stay in that job or move on is ultimately yours.

The more you learn from the position you're in now, the more skills and knowledge you'll take to the next interview, job, or opportunity. And if you're in one of those sticky spots where you have to ride it out for a while before you can effectively leave this job for one with more opportunity and fewer asshats, then at least try to make the time in career purgatory worthwhile by learning as much as you can and using your spare time to explore options for the future.

And though I wish I could tell you that you can skip or rush through the process of going from the worst job ever to the best career you could possibly imagine, you just can't. You're going to make mistakes, and you're going to make enemies along the way. That's one of the hardest lessons I think, at least it is for me. You can try to be Miss Congeniality all you want, and you can even be a genuinely good person and awesome asset to the company, but there will still be people who don't like you and don't want the best for you.

Whether they're jealous, petty, or just mad at the whole world and taking it out on you, try to keep your attitude positive, and don't let their bad attitude or obnoxious

behavior drag you down. Whenever possible, follow the Michelle Obama directive, "When they go low, we go high," because your integrity and credibility are extremely difficult to reclaim once you've allowed yourself to be dragged into drama.

Now, I don't know what your eventual goal is in career or life, but I do have confidence that if you've chosen to read this and gotten this far, you're likely pretty committed to success and finding a way to turn bad jobs into good skills. I'm genuinely grateful that you have chosen to let me guide you through the first part of that process, and I'm also truly interested in hearing from you to find out what you learned and where the lessons you learned from this obsequious opus might take you. You can reach me at **www.wendydwyer.com**.

Good luck, and best wishes for a totally awesome, fulfilling, and rewarding career.

Wendy Dwyer

Acknowledgements

While it may be true that a whole bunch of a writer's life is spent hunched over a keyboard with only the tap, tap, tapping sounds of the keys to keep her company, it's also true that none of us is an island – even when we want to be.

We write because we want to be heard, listened to, and because we have something we feel is important to share. If not for the encouragement and support of a host of others, this book would not have been possible. And while I may forget to mention you by name, please know I really am grateful, and you can blame the memory lapse on the stiff neck from being hunched over a keyboard for months on end.

I appreciate the extra assistance from Anne Alexander, whose gentle proofreading kept me from crying myself to sleep over stupid mistakes.

I am eternally grateful to the wonderful Carrie Sills from ArtWithCare.com, who said yes to working with me again after all these years and three Category Four hurricanes.

I owe a debt of gratitude to colleagues Marvin Hobson, Tiffany Lewis, and April Van Camp for convincing me I can do anything and that I have something to say.

I am so grateful for the editors and English teachers in my past who encouraged me to write. If it weren't for you, I'd still be standing on my twin bed, dreaming of getting a gig as the Texaco Star girl, singing, "You can trust your car to the man who wears the star – the big bright Texaco star!"

To my students, thank you for making me feel like I have something of value to share.

To my family, my dad, mom, brother, niece, nephew, and favorite aunt (Dee), thank you for not giving up on me – ever.

To the bosses, good and bad, great coworkers and asshats in my storied employment history, thank you for teaching me something in every job and at every step of the journey.

Above all, I'm in awe of my husband, Dan, who not only believes I can do anything, but usually helps me to prove it to myself, too.

About the Author

Wendy Dwyer has had a wide variety of employment experiences (translation – a lot of strange jobs). She has worked with phenomenally talented individuals and suffered her share of asshats, too. An Associate Professor at Indian River State College, she also writes for local and regional publications, spotlighting events, volunteers, and non-profit activities.

An award-winning writer, educator, creative consultant, and public relations professional with a boundless imagination and knack for creating wildly-successful fundraising ideas and events, Dwyer also provides dynamic and engaging public relations trainings for organizations and businesses. When she is not working or volunteering, she enjoys writing, walking, and spending time with her husband Dan and a large variety of rescued animals at her rural home in Fort Pierce, Florida.

Made in the USA
Columbia, SC
24 September 2017